In a Drea

I came across a wood in the clear of night.
A freshly fallen snow, a blanket of white.
From afar I could see in moonlight plain as day,
a worn and trodden bridge, a well-beaten
pathway.
As my feet they did follow, smoke curled above
the trees.
A glow of fire put my soul at ease.
A fox I did see, a peculiar sight,
sitting alone by the glow of the light.
"Come, come," the fox, he did say.
"I have watched you in your waking day.
My, how you wonder. My, how you dream.
All that you stand for. All that you beam.
It is, of course, fortunate for you -
your every last wish in life will come true."
And then he did hand me a cup full of cheer
And toasted his own and shouted, "Here, here!"
As I drank, a sensation it did grow,
the ground where I stood began to sink from
below.
Awake there I was, safe in my bed.
A pattering heart, a throbbing head.
To the window I did rise, drawing the curtain
back

to see a curl of smoke in the moonlit black.

A Stirring of Leaves

A stirring of leaves, a breaking of wood.
My heart it grieves, of that it should.
I have lost you, like the moon behind a cloud.
If only I knew, to keep what I had vowed.
On these cold lonely nights, my bed remains bare.
My dreams are haunted by what we once did share.
I never meant to let you slip so far away.
For the sake of us, I wish you chose to stay.

Come Away

My love, I miss you. Will it ever be?
I dream of you in a far off land, a place where we are free.
Your smiling eyes, oh, those eyes, the ones I do adore.
In a distant future, I've seen them there before.
How happy we are in that time, living it up, my dear.
Where there is no worry, where there is no fear.
We dance by fire light, the world is only ours.
My, how I love you there, more than all the stars.
Can it ever be, my dear?
Our future and what I see so clear?
Let us wait no longer, let us start tonight.
Our bodies close, our dreams come true, what a wondrous sight.
Take my hand, take my heart, come away with me.
Let us live this life, let us find the key.

Shattered

How could I have known, you'd shatter?
If only I'd known, I would've held you
in my arms a little more.
Let the sun fall on you.
I would've tried to keep you, to carry you.
But oh, you were already gone.
You were already gone.
All the love I had in me,
was yours to light the days.
And what a comfort that has been.
But now, we're worlds apart.
You're in my mind,
you're in my heart,
I'll keep a part of you,
always and ever.
You shattered into pieces.
And I? I did the same.

An Ending

I have wandered far, the trees now covered in
snow.
The bright light that I saw has all but sunk
below.
My footsteps are lost, and paths are now unseen,
for the white covers that which I do not see.
In the pocket of my coat, is placed a single page
for you.
My last letter home, the last words to see me
through.
I fear not if this is the end.
For all I want to do is see you again.
For only a glimpse of life is all that I lack.
Oh, I could stay here, but it wouldn't bring you
back.

Let Me Wander With You

Let me wander with you,
into the haze of forever.
Let me wander with you,
to a place where hearts can endeavor.
Let me wander with you,
to a realm where souls can feel.
Let me wander with you,
to a time when we both can heal.
Let me wander with you,
through the midst of paradise.
Let me wander with you,
where our love is not a sacrifice.
Let me wander with you,
in those eyes so blue.

Please, My Love

In my final moments on this Earth you held me close.
To see my face again I know you long for most.
I am safe, I am loved, on this side I feel no pain.
I patiently await for the day I see you again.
But please, my love, for me do not despair.
Your heartbreak turned to action, of that I could not bear.
I have seen the coming days, so bright and so true.
You will go on to love again, I wish you only knew.
These words I hope you find,
in the winds of your mind.
I will always love you,
until the end of time.
And there I will wait until the very end of you.
But please, my love, don't do what you can't undo.

In the Morning

Sun kissed morning light,
awakes my soul, shiny and bright.
Of this day I give thanks and praise.
A joy I hope always stays.
These words of affirmation I do say aloud.
I am grateful, never hateful, of myself I am proud.
When I think back of what I've done along the way,
I am filled with peace as it brought me to this day.
A day where I love the person I have grown to be.
A day where I am weightless, a day where I am free.
All the darkness of the past,
has no place here, it simply cannot last.
As the sun it rises, chasing out the night.
So too my heart sings of all that is right.

By the Mystic Moon

By the mystic moon, I do walk the night.
The love I once knew is gone without a fight.
Pale frost nips the twigs of December.
Who I was before us, do you remember?
I cannot recall, it's been so long.
Where did we go wrong?
Where I lost you, I did not see.
Years of loving you have changed the heart of me.
By the bank of the river, I hear an owl sing.
As the moon rises, I know not what the night will bring.
The moon is beautiful, just like you.
How to gain you back, I wish I knew.
If only you were here to take me by the hand.
I wish we could have done all that we had planned.

Welcome, Little Boy

Emerald mountains of forest, a sleepy little town.
A quiet life of solitude, a story of how I drowned.
Nobody was there to see it, nobody in the night.
A night, that had no memory, no memory of the light.
The old clock, it rang the hour of my death.
I looked up and saw it as I took my last breath.
It was the first time that the old clock had rang.
A nightmare, a bright flash and suddenly, bang.
I am reborn, I am reborn.
I cry out as my last life I still mourn.
I feel arms wrap around me, a mother's pure delight.
"I have waited so long for you; I never gave up the fight."
The words she spoke to me through her tears of joy,
soothed my soul as she continued, "Welcome, little boy."

Amongst the Trees

Amongst the trees I wander, an old haunt when in need.
Fierce and strong, they protect me; let me stop and bleed.
For here amongst the twigs and moss and leaves of yesterday,
I can hang my head and cry or simply stop to pray.
I think of things, I wish for things, I feel things I thought lost.
I wash away my worries, nothing does it cost.
In any kind of season, on any kind of day,
I know what I pour here, amongst the trees it will stay.
Saying not a word, whispering only wind,
the trees I know they stand for me, no matter how I've sinned.
How is it possible? How can that be?
How a wood can cleanse me, set my soul at ease.
There must be something magic, something old and wise.
Of the Earth, of the skies, amongst the trees it lies.

Before I Knew You

I loved you before I knew you.
I knew you before I saw you.
Before I even knew your name,
your laughter, your face.
I loved you before I knew you.
Now, I know your name.
I know your laugh.
I know your face.
There is nothing
that could ever take your place.
I love you now.
I loved you then.
I love you still.
I always will.

For Her

Easy in manner, elegant, refined.
Most difficult to properly define.
An homage to her loveliness.
My love for her, how can I express?
Loving unselfishly her kin and kind,
yet to her own rare merits ever blind.
Sweeter than air with a fairer face,
owning her glamor, owning her grace.
Cherry lips and sparkling eyes,
hair in twisted locks that shines.
Born beneath a lucky star,
radiant her beauties are.
With no faults she leaves me charmed,
to her captivation I am unarmed.

The Soul of Me and You

I dream of our own pathway
somewhere far and away,
to a world in which we share
love of a deep care
where only we dare
to take a chance
and exchange a glance
at the soul of me and you.

In a Field of Grass

In a field of grass, like silken hair,
at midday in a summer breeze.
The dew has dried from the wildflowers
as honeybees meander.
We sit with no words and watch the trees
as clouds blow across the land.
It is here that the memory of you blooms.
And it is here that my heart drinks you in.

I Heard

I heard what they said of this place,
I heard the words spoke before me for thousands
of years.
I heard that if you look at all that exists in your
life,
all that you already are, all that you already
have:
air to breathe, music to hear,
books to read, stars to dream by,
friends to love and places to go.
You are richer than you will ever know.
And never in one lifetime could you spend it all.

Keys to the World

There is nothing so small,
no thought however fleeting
no task mindlessly done
no word unspoken and nevèr reaching,
that it is not sent into the unseen,
touching the heart of hearts,
where it echoes and comes back more of the
same.
And as manifestations are called into your life,
you'll come to see that there is no detail too
small.
You hold the keys to the world.

Ever So

You see ever so far,
there in the vast is eternity.
You count ever so much,
there is infinity beyond that.
Do not be impatient.
We have time still.
Wider and wider they go, ever so.
And yet, there will always be enough.

By the Blue Shore

By the blue shore
I dreamed of peace,
peace that would never come.
By the blue shore
I yearned for love,
love that was nevermore.
By the blue shore
I mourned my loss,
loss of life never lived.
By the blue shore
I dreamed of anew,
a better future, one free from you.

Living Fire

At the edge of a wood
there is a fire burning bright.
I've never seen a light like it before.
From a distance my heart starts yearning.
I'm lured by the heat and the light of it.
As I get closer I can feel the heat on my face.
I need to be near, I need to reach it's flames.
My trodden path is just ahead.
A crow, sitting on the ground.
"Come child and be at ease.
Sit and rest inside the heat.
See the light in the flames,
as it dances, twirls and glows.
Watch the way it chases everything away.
For I come, in my many and myriad forms.
The moon, the sun and the stars.
All that you see before your eyes.
They are I, the one true living fire."

As the Cold Wind Howled

By the light of the moon
I saw a fox run by
And I chased it, I chased it
With excitement and fury
For I love to run
And the fox, it ran away
Through the pine and through the oak
And I followed it, I followed it
And I quivered for those challenges
As we tore through the forest
And the fox it ran and ran
Until there was no end to the snow covered field
And I still chased it, I chased it
Until the frozen sky I reached
Flying to the moon
Walking on the stars
I landed upon a white frozen peak
And again I saw the fox
But this time I paused, I paused
Above the glistening snow
as the cold wind howled.

www.ingramcontent.com/pod-product-compliance
Lightning Source LLC
Chambersburg PA
CBHW051721130826
49812CB00034B/1281
* 9 7 8 9 3 5 7 2 1 3 1 4 1 *